# HELPING YOU THROUGH LOSS AND BEREAVEMENT

**Natural** First Aid for the Soul in Grief.

David Griffiths

Copyright © 2024 Deibachdrwsnesa

All rights reserved. Without limiting the rights under the copyright reserved above, no part of this publication may be reproduced, stored in, or introduced into a retrieval system, or transmitted in any form or by any means (electronic, mechanical, photocopying, recording, or otherwise) without prior written permission.

For permission requests, please contact: bydbacheihun@songwriter.net

While every effort has been made to ensure the accuracy and legitimacy of the references, referrals, and links (collectively "Links") presented in this book, deibachdrwsnesa is not responsible or liable for broken Links or missing or fallacious information at the Links. Any Links in this book to a specific product, process, website, or service do not constitute or imply an endorsement by deibachdrwsnesa of same, or its producer or provider. The views and opinions contained at any Links do not necessarily express or reflect those of deibachdrwsnesa.

# Contents

Introduction ..................................................................................... 2
Chapter 1: This Book Is For You ................................................. 6
Chapter 2.: Bodily Health ............................................................ 19
Chapter 3: Emotional Health ....................................................... 35
Chapter 4: Spiritual Health. ......................................................... 41
Chapter 5: The stages of grief and two models of grief .............. 45
Chapter 6: Grief and Bereavement as significant stages on the spiritual path. ......................................................................... 52
Chapter 7: Helpful links .............................................................. 57
Chapter 8: Poems and writings about grief and loss. .................. 61

"Our birth is but a sleep and a forgetting:
The Soul that rises with us, our life's Star,
Hath had elsewhere its setting,
And cometh from afar:
Not in entire forgetfulness,
And not in utter nakedness,
But trailing clouds of glory do we come
From God, who is our home:
Heaven lies about us in our infancy!
Shades of the prison-house begin to close
Upon the growing Boy,
But he beholds the light, and whence it flows,
He sees it in his joy;"

Fragment from;
'Ode: Intimations of Immortality':
A Poem by William Wordsworth

# Introduction

Hello.

I'm glad you've found this book on *Natural* First Aid for the grieving soul. You've come to the right place, and this is why;

The emphasis of this book is on how to weather the stormy seas of grief in a *natural* way and how this process is so important for You, on your own journey through life.

For many years, I have been a volunteer for the U.K. bereavement service CRUSE, and for four years I have been a supervisor for CRUSE.

During that time I have helped hundreds of clients and volunteers safely through the process of bereavement.

With the skills, knowledge and techniques gathered over that time I'd like to share these with a wider audience and thus help many more people through the challenges of grief and bereavement.

As well as my counselling work I have had profound personal experiences of bereavement.

During the early Covid years of 2019 - 2021, I lost four close family members including my dear mother. There is nothing like personal experience to help put ourselves in the place of another.

As I had spent much of my retirement helping to care for my mother and her two sisters, who have subsequently died, I felt loss, emptiness, uncertainty about the future and some lack of purpose as I had seen my purpose in life mainly as being a good parent to my two daughters and to look after the elderly members of my family.

As a family we experienced a touch of grace as one of my daughters gave birth to a beautiful little girl. Fortunately, a few weeks before she passed, my mother was able to meet her great granddaughter. This was a doubly joyful experience as not only did they manage to meet in time but the secret of my granddaughter's name was revealed to her great grandmother, and it was her own name – Ella.

It was heartwarming and touching to see the expression on my mother's face when she was told what name her great granddaughter had been given. She was in such disbelief that she thought my daughter was joking when she told her the name. Tears came to her eyes but, being of the old fashioned type, she quickly regained her composure and her smile beamed across the room.

In the event becoming a grandfather was one of the greatest events in my life and allowed me to be a carer once more, but this time at the opposite end of the spectrum!

Something else of note on a personal level is the way that the Robin has always appeared to me shortly after a bereavement. Of course there are always Robins about, but not often do they sit stock still not far away from you and retain eye contact for several minutes. This has happened to me so many times that now I've come to expect to see the Robin and to engage in this vision space

*Helping You Through Loss and Bereavement*

whenever there has been a close bereavement. Others will see white feathers or other symbols which give them a feeling that the deceased is still with them, and this is extremely comforting.

The focus of this book is on emotional first aid for the bereaved. I believe if you carry out the suggestions given, you will gain a sense of acceptance and peace around your loss.

At the end of each chapter in the physical book format, there are blank pages on which to make notes or attach photographs, articles etcetera.

For those using an electronic format, please access a blank journal or notebook for the same purpose.

At the end of the book there are links to helpful organisations, websites, publications etc. in the U.K. There will be similar organizations in other countries and you will be able to find them through an Internet search engine.

However, as this is meant to be a short book on "natural first aid", I have reduced any other information to a minimum and shall deal with practical issues in the book; "Practicalities Around Death and Bereavement" which gives a step by step guide to what to do when someone dies.

Chapter 1 looks at soul healing, followed by 2,3, and 4 which, in turn, focus on improving your Physical, Emotional and Spiritual health. Chapter 5 looks at the stages of grief and two models of grief and Chapter 6 looks at Grief and Bereavement on the path of personal evolution, or spiritual path.

Chapter 7 provides links to helpful organisations and Chapter 8 contains poems and writings to help ease you through your grief and may be used for eulogies.

# CHAPTER 1

# This Book Is For You

---※---

It is here for you to use as a support during your grieving process. Right now you are hurting and need, not so much a book on the practicalities of coping with the duties of a bereavement, but emotional first aid and a solid understanding of what's going on for you.

In book 2, if you wish, you can learn about cancelling bank accounts, pension payments, newspaper deliveries etc. etc.

You will learn about funerals, probate and Inquests.

But right now you're missing your beloved.

Keeping busy is a well-known way of distracting you from your grief and although it can be a useful tactic at times, it's not a long term solution.

*Let's take a look at what really happened;*

Have you noticed that when you interact with different people that you assume a different character? A different tone of voice? Different expressions?

This means that for every one you encounter you adopt a different character.

What happens when the person that you were used to encountering is no longer there physically in front of you, what does your character do, the character that was used to engaging with your beloved, what does it do?

The answer is shocking; that part of you feels as though it is dying!

Depending on how close you were to the deceased, to your beloved, then it will be a very large or a smaller part of you and thus a very large or a smaller trauma.

What does this character do now that your beloved has passed away?

The answer to this is *it feels as though it is dying*. Therefore when your beloved passed away there were two deaths occurring; one was the death of the beloved and the other the death of the part of you that used to interact with them.

We interact in a particular way, with a particular set of memories, emotions and actions with each individual we meet. Put together, this psychological complex is known as a "character".

Close your eyes for a minute and imagine some of the people you know well. Now become aware of how you feel. In your mind's eye slowly picture five or six of these people, including your beloved who has passed and sense how you feel as you move from one to another. These feelings and thoughts and facial expressions etc. that you experience as you move from one to the next are called "characters" or "parts". Each person evokes a different "part" in you.

When you're not thinking about the person the part is still there, in the unconscious mind, awaiting a call. What happens when the call never comes, as when the "matching" person has died? That part feels **abandoned**.

My work here is to help you in a kind and compassionate way to make a new relationship with your loved one, as I have done over many years of counselling clients with CRUSE, the bereavement charity.

This will help to alleviate your grief.

This is worth repeating;

**This will help to alleviate your grief.**

It will help you to feel better, it will help you to cope with the loss and it will help you to begin to feel joy once more in your life.

How do we "save" the part which is dying, feels abandoned?

## We create a new relationship with the Beloved.

Some might call it a *spiritual* relationship, or a *soul* relationship. The point is that the abandoned part need not die, it simply needs to transform the relationship with the beloved.

What follows does not imply concepts such as an afterlife, continuation of the soul after death etc. and is free of any religious belief.

It is simply a helping hand held out to YOU.

This is the emotional first aid and should be observed in a <u>*mood of calm and reverence*</u>;

<u>(If you feel you are unable to do this, perhaps because of some issue you had with the deceased, then please skip this exercise and maybe return at a time when the issue is of less emotional weight).</u>

1. Find a place at home where you can sit in quiet without being disturbed at some time of the day. For most people this is usually the evening but it can be early morning or it can be both.

2. Make sure that you will not be disturbed in your quiet place. Turn the phone and television off. If you can't find such a space then there are other options available. It may be that you can find somewhere safe and quiet to walk for 20 minutes or so before your day begins, before you start work or at the end of the day - somewhere quiet and safe to walk before you return home.

3. The point is to create an opportunity where you think of, and connect with, your beloved for 20 minutes or half an hour or more every day.

4. Preparation at home; If you are able to sit in a quiet and uninterrupted place at home then see if you can find a small table upon which you place a nice clean and special cloth, perhaps in your beloved's favourite colour and on this cloth place a candle. Also on the cloth you could place a picture or pictures of your beloved; crystals, shells, personal items which were special to them and/or to yourself. Additionally you may have some letters which you wrote to the beloved or which they wrote to you or possibly a poem or poems which they loved to read or loved to hear.

5. You will soon collect some precious items for your special table. In addition you may have a piece of music which was their favourite and you may wish to play this music during this part of the day. At some stage, especially if you are able to sit in silence, you will begin to feel the presence of the beloved. Please do not be disturbed by this. It is very natural for bereaved persons to feel the presence of the one who has passed, even to hear their voice and sometimes even to catch glimpses of them. I repeat - this is perfectly normal and usual for bereaved people to experience. This is an opportunity for you, that is, the part of you which feels as though life has no meaning, to live again in a new way in a new relationship with the loved one. At this point you may choose to read a poem or a

letter or a spiritual script which you feel will be helpful for your beloved. If so take your time, consider the words that you are reading and dwell on them for a while. Try to make sure that the words you are reading are uplifting, of a high vibration, of a healthy energy.

6. This is where the healing takes place. To the extent to which you engage in this practice then to the same extent you will be able to help yourself and others of your family or friends who are also grieving.

*A personal anecdote may help here;*

*In my work as a bereavement volunteer for CRUSE I once was helping a nurse, a young lady who had lost her mother recently. This young lady worked in the intensive care ward at the local hospital. She was very concerned that she might break down in tears during her working day. Not only would this be inappropriate but might also be of concern to her colleagues as she was nursing very ill patients.*

*I explained to her that if, during the day, she felt she was going to break down, she need only remind herself that later that evening she would spend half an hour in a quiet space in connection with her mother. Not only would she be able to cry her eyes out and express her grief fully* **before** *sitting with her mother but this would be an event to look forward to, something very special and rare in life. This knowledge would allow her to postpone the crying and breaking down from the work day and the work place to the evening, where it would be totally appropriate; followed by the peaceful "tuning in" time.*

If you are unable to find a quiet and uninterrupted space at home then you might immerse yourself in the loving feeling for the beloved during a walk or possibly while sitting on a park bench or even in your car. The location should always be safe of course.

You could take a briefcase or a bag with you containing the cloth, candles, crystals, poetry etc. and take these out appropriately at your destination and thereby connect lovingly with the one who has passed.

A walk may be to a favourite place where you and your special person used to walk together or where they used to walk alone.

The point is that the environment which you create should bring about a peaceful and joyful feeling of connection with your beloved.

Another excellent technique is to write a letter or a journal to your loved one explaining the events of your life and this could be an ongoing practice.

After a few days of communing in this way you will find that you will look forward to these events.

No relationship is perfect and it may be that there were some issues between yourself and the one who has passed. However, this is not the time to think those thoughts. Now is the time to accompany the loved one with loving thoughts and feelings. Happy times when you shared your lives together, times when you supported each other, made important telephone calls etc.

After a few weeks you may decide to make this connection every other day or once a week as your judgment requires.

Just as you yourself are climbing the next mountain in your life and raising yourself to a higher view, a clearer view, so will the feeling of the deceased move on and you will find after a period of five or six weeks that the connection becomes naturally thinner.

This leads to an important point. At the end of each session you should say the following words;

*"I let go of you as you let go of me and we shall meet again in the Fields of Peace."*

The use of these words avoids any undue dependency upon the deceased and leads to a healthy situation.

## Helpful practices.

Just to repeat;

This book is for YOU . It is here for you to use as a support during your grieving process. I am here to help you as I have done for hundreds of clients over many years of bereavement counselling.

After you have felt the presence of your beloved during the times put aside, for a period of days or a few weeks, you may wish to try the following practice.

## Grounding.

One problem that many people complain of whilst grieving is that of an uncontrolled mind, the monkey mind as it is known.

This mind is often uncontrollable at the best of times but when you are stressed as after a bereavement then the uncontrolled mind often has a field day.

*I once had a lady client, in her sixties, who had lost her much-loved father. She would visit the grave often but found herself sitting on a nearby bench, often as darkness fell, unable to leave. When we explored this, she explained that she couldn't bear to leave him alone and cold in the grave.*

*With gentle prompting, she came to realise that, whatever her father's situation, he would be unable to be aware of a lonely and cold existence around a body which was no longer alive.*

*This is an example of the tricks and delusions of the mind.*

How to deal with this "monkey mind"?

A very simple and very effective exercise is as follows;

Sit comfortably with your back fairly upright, ensuring you are warm and safe and will not be disturbed by people or phones etc.

Close your eyes and simply *feel your feet.*

You may also become aware of the place where your body sits on the seat and of your clothes on your skin etc.

The process here is that energy follows the attention. Therefore if you place the attention on the feet or the lower body in general, the energy is drawn away from the head and thereby the thoughts and inner conversations are starved of energy.

Without attention the thoughts and inner chattering cannot continue. The activities of the mind depend upon the energy provided through attention.

Now move the attention up the body, gradually releasing tensions as you go, not forgetting the arms. When you reach the top of the head try to feel the body as a whole. Each time you do this you will be relieved to find that the mind calms down, you will have a much needed break! The more you practice the easier it becomes and the more effective it becomes.

That's it!

This may seem too simple to be true as is often the case with mental hygiene. All you need to do is practice this exercise and you will find that the thoughts and chattering gradually come to an end, at least for the period of the practice.

Then you will be free from the tyranny of the mind and this will be of enormous benefit to you and to your mental health.

In addition you may wish to practice the following;

1. Walking in a safe environment, place your attention on something about 50 yards or so in front of you. The object needs to stand out from the background to a certain extent in order to make focusing easier. For example a bright bush or plants in the near distance or a coloured stone or structure which easily stands out from the background.

As you walk towards the object keeping your focus upon it, say to yourself inwardly *"seeing, seeing, seeing"* and become aware of the process and sense of vision.

This will result in a clear mind and eventually in the capacity to stand back from your experiences and become less reactive and therefore less anxious.

2. In addition, when you have mastered this exercise you can add another element which is to *feel your feet* on the ground as you are walking, as you are focusing and as you are repeating inwardly *"seeing, seeing, seeing."*

3. One more simple exercise to help you keep your mind clear will complete the hat trick.

This exercise relies upon using either a mantra consisting of words or of a song or tune which lifts your mood.

The mantra can be some wise words from scripture or from a poem or from a favourite contemporary spiritual teacher. e.g. Mooji;

*"Focus on your Heart - until you and your Heart are the same."*

This can be your mantra, which you can repeat inwardly over and over.

Mooji goes on to explain;

*"When you focus on presence, there is a vibration there.*

*Stay in that vibration.*

*No time to think or do.*

*Do not engage in such mindless thoughts.*

*Gradually, an energy is held here (in the heart). This energy transforms into a powerful field of silence, joy, love.*

*Your mind interest is fading.*

*Don't follow the flow of the mind.*

*The mind will use different techniques to get your attention. Just stay quiet (silently)*

*Keep doing what you're doing in your life, but isolate some moments to sit and be in this indivisible state. This state will expand.*

*This is everything! "*

The song can be a favourite popular song. In my case I know that The Beach Boys "I can hear music" or "Good Vibrations" or

Roger Hodgson's "Give a Little Bit" always do the trick also there are more recent songs which have the same uplifting effect.

Of course the works of Mozart and other classical composers can also be very uplifting.

There you have it, a hat-trick of exercises to help you keep your mind free of circling thoughts, inner conversations, imaginings, and daydreams.

Why is this important in terms of grieving?

Because your feelings are usually the result of your thoughts. If you can take a break from negative thoughts through the above exercises, you will begin to feel better and make your way carefully and safely through your grief.

At times, you may want to sit with your grief and allow yourself to feel all the feelings that come up, from sadness, anger, hopelessness to joy, optimism, relief etc. – **whatever arises is o.k.** and gradually you will feel yourself as an observer of your emotions, rather than being a victim of them.

In the next three chapters we shall look at the importance of maintaining bodily, emotional and spiritual health.

# CHAPTER 2

# Bodily Health

---

This is the basis of our earthly existence and it is so important that you;

1. Keep yourself and environment clean.
2. Eat good food and regular meals.
3. Keep yourself and your home warm and comfortable.
4. Take excercise (enjoyable too).
5. Give your body some tender loving care.
6. Continue with dental and medical appointments etc.
7. Financial health is included under this heading and at the end of the book I have included links to institutions which can help with financial difficulties.
8. Contact with the Earth, gardening, barefoot walking etc.

Whatever your life situation; you may be young and single, older and single, living with others, living alone, living with parents, in student accommodation, in a home for the elderly, in nursing care, or any other life condition, the principles above apply to all situations and will help you to traverse the rough waters of the bereavement voyage.

## Taking each point in turn;

1. The point about keeping clean is that it makes you feel better and it makes your environment feel better so please continue to take regular showers or baths and continue to clean your home. If during this time you feel unable to hoover the floors or to wash down the surfaces etc. then, if you can afford it, consider hiring someone to clean for you in the short term until you come through this difficult period. Perhaps a family member would agree to clean the house for you in return for a meal or whatever you might decide.

2. This is probably not a good time to change your diet. Your body is already going through lots of changes as a result of changing emotions so be kind to yourself, eat whatever food you like to eat and then when you come through this, you might want to look at your diet, how to improve it and even how to reduce spending on food.

    For now the best thing to do is to treat yourself to your favourite foods.

3. Keeping warm is most important as your soul already feels as though it is in a cold space, so make sure that your environment is comfortably warm. Go to bed in a warm bed and ensure that you wake up to a warm house. Keeping your house warm need not be expensive. Just to repeat; your soul feels isolated, bereft and cold and so it is important that you keep your body warm as this then reflects back on the soul.

4. Take exercise. Here is a tip which is very important; *the quickest way to relieve mental and emotional anguish is through exercise.* This is a quick and effective way of feeling better. However the benefits will only last for a few days then you will need to go back to the exercise once more.

Imagine a bucket overflowing with water. This is your soul when over filled with emotion. If you can partly or completely empty the bucket then there will be more room in your soul for emotions without them overflowing and resulting in a tearful breakdown.

## Exercise will empty your bucket.

You may already be a fit person with a regular exercise routine. In which case just continue with your current plan.

If you're not used to exercising then you can use this period of bereavement not only to pay your respects to your beloved one but also to improve your body fitness.

Whichever exercise you decide to start it is important that you consult your health professional before beginning any exercise plan if you are already suffering from illness.

There are many options before you so let's start with the easiest and assume that you're not used to exercising and that you need to build up slowly to a regular routine.

Probably the easiest way and the least strenuous exercise is **rebounding.** According to NASA, the American space agency, rebounding is the most efficient exercise ever devised by the human race. The reason for this is that every cell in your body is exercised during the bounce on the rebounder. At the top of the bounce all of the cells are more or less weightless whereas at the bottom of the bounce each cell experiences maximum gravity. Therefore during each bounce each cell experiences the range of expansion and contraction from weightlessness to maximum gravity.

Even if you are unable to use the rebounder in the usual way you can still rest your feet on the surface and bounce your legs up and down. At least this will exercise the muscles in your legs and improve circulation.

There are many kinds and sizes of rebounder available. They vary in price from around £50 to over £100. If you have problems with your balance there are rebounders available with hand grips at waist height so that you can hold on whilst bouncing. As well as being a great way to maintain fitness rebounding is also good fun! You can bounce as much and as vigorously and for as long as you like. It's up to you! It is usually a good idea to at least become a bit breathless as this achieves the goal of reducing your "emotional voltage.".

Other activities include walking, jogging, swimming, dancing, Tai Chi, aerobics, Yoga etc. You may want to become a member of a local gymnasium and swimming pool.

*David Griffiths*

# REBOUNDER.

## Tip;

There is nothing wrong with the way you feel. People react in different ways to bereavement. **However you feel is ok.**

Emotional
Bucket FULL!
Emotions overflow;

After Exercise, room for more emotions.

Emotions no longer overflow.

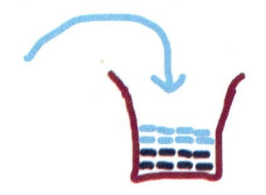

If you need to really let the tears flow and find this embarrassing then this can be done inconspicuously in the shower or whilst walking or jogging in a downpour of rain.

Before you engage in any of these activities you may wish to consult your health professional.

5. TLC; The body and mind affect one another. If your emotions are strong over a period of time this may show up as fatigue or illness in the body. Likewise if the body is well looked after this will have a positive effect on the mind. There are many "body treats" available these days, quite often available at hotels with spa pools and saunas. Or how about a new hair style? Whatever it is it will be good to have something to look forward to and to enjoy, possibly with a friend?

6. Continue with dental and medical appointments etc. This clearly makes sense and requires no further elaboration.

7. Financial Health. Quite often those "left behind" may have been partly, or to a great extent, financially dependent upon the deceased. There may also be issues around paying for the funeral, sale of property, issues around the will etc. Whilst you are grieving you really won't want to engage in these matters, especially if you are dealing with them alone. Therefore I have included links at the end of the book to show what help is available - you are NOT alone!

8. Contact with the Earth, soil, trees, forest walks.

## Contact with the Earth.

[What follows is gleaned mainly from the excellent work of Sadhguru and the Isha Foundation, and other sources.] [Italicised lines are quotes from Sadhguru].

As you will be acutely aware at this time, in one way or another we all return to the soil. This is an opportunity to ponder your own mortality, how do you intend spending the rest of your life? What's the most benefit you can be to society, your family and friends, yourself?

*"If you are close to the earth, you are constantly being reminded that you are mortal – physiologically, on the cellular level, and on the elemental level. This reminder of mortality is the most key element in your spiritual process. You would long to know something beyond the body only because you know it will end one day. If this body was immortal, who would sit and meditate, who would want to know anything beyond this? Even if you are not consciously aware, somewhere deep down, you know that your expiry date is on."*

Perhaps your bereavement has caused you to consider some major questions, "what's it all about?", "who am I really, behind the actors and the characters?"

Most of all, how can I find answers to these questions? Is there anyone out there who knows the answers – truly?

If you find yourself asking these questions, may I suggest the works of Mooji, Sadhguru and Wendell Henckel?

At his ashram [retreat, community] in India, Sadhguru advises his students to immerse their hands in soil, sticky soil, for at least an hour every day. Not so easy in UK, European or US climes you may think, but keen gardeners do this all year 'round, and aren't they amongst the healthiest and most robust members of society?

We live our lives unconsciously, unaware of the elements surrounding us. The elements of space, air, light and fire, water and earth. Preoccupied with thoughts and activities we take the elements for granted and use them in a functional way.

Nearly everybody lives in their own mindset of thoughts, feelings and plans for the future, as well as memories, which can take up all our attention.

Our education is designed to make us think of our surroundings as "resources" in an exploitative manner. Hence the ecological crisis facing humanity in this day and age. For example in India the damming of rivers and cutting down of trees on the shores of the riverbanks has resulted in some rivers, during the summer, not being able to reach the sea.

*"What you call as your body is just a piece of the planet. If you lose connection with the source, you will get disorganized. Fitness and wellbeing does not mean walking on a treadmill and having bulging muscles. It is very important to strengthen the integrity of the elements in our system. There are specific methods with which we can do this."*

*The Earth is the basis of life. The more you are in touch with it, it is better. If your hands and your bare feet are in contact with the earth, it will harmonize the physiological process in your system. Whenever it is in contact with the earth, the body reorganizes itself. Try to spend at least a few minutes a day in the garden, barefoot, touching plants or trees. This is a simple way to connect with the earth.*

*This contact with nature, whether its earth, air or water is most important. Without this contact, the body will slowly lose its integrity and its stability. It may still survive, it may not die tomorrow morning, but it loses a variety of capabilities that it has come with. The possibilities that the human system carries is lost as you lose contact with the natural elements.*

Sadhguru describes seven ways of making contact with the earth;

1. Bare hands and/or feet touching the earth. Walking barefoot on the soil or touching soil, plants or trees with our bare hands. At least walking barefoot indoors if not possible outside.

2. Earthing. Lying on the ground in the prone position with bare skin or wet clothes touching the earth.

3. Walking barefoot or sitting on the floor, especially during New Moons, when the Moon's gravity is least and you're more likely to feel a *conscious* connection with the earth.

4. Walking barefoot for at least half an hour before lunch or dinner – the digestion is improved.

5. Sleeping on, or close to, the floor. [for a period of time]. *"If you have a very unstable body and tend to fall sick very easily, just get off your bed or cot and sleep on the floor. It*

*will make a big difference. If you get just eighteen inches closer to the earth, you will see that it will make big difference in terms of reorganizing the system. I would say eighty percent of your health depends on how much in tune you are with the earth. Eighty percent of your chronic ailments can just vanish, simply because you found a little rapport with the earth on which you are walking or sitting right now."*

6. 6.Awareness of the five elements; Space, Air, Light/heat, Water and Earth. Sadhguru recommends becoming aware of these elements during the day. Become aware of Space through the sense of hearing, Air through the sense of touch, Light through the sense of vision, Water through the sense of taste and Earth through the sense of smell. Take time during the day to experience that every time you breathe or eat or drink something you are taking in a part of the Earth and its atmosphere.

7. Bury your feet in the earth. *"There are ways of getting more involved with the planet all of us live on and are made of. If you have a garden and some privacy, after you finish your sadhana in the morning, dig a hole in your backyard that is about two feet deep. Put your feet inside, close the hole up to just above your ankles, and stay there for thirty to forty minutes, simply stuck in the earth. There are many benefits to this practice. In terms of health, you will see that if you attune yourself to the ways of the planet, allergies will vanish. Fundamentally, allergies indicate*

*that something within you is not in rapport with the life-making material of this planet."*

In addition Sadhguru explains how sleeping with your head to the North is out of harmony with the Earth's magnetic field and is not a good idea.

Because the earth is packed full of electrons, when you touch the earth with your bare skin you have access to all of these electrons which can bring electrical balance to your body and thus improve your health.

When grounded you will immediately feel better.

Just as all electrical appliances need to be earthed, not only for safety's sake but also to prevent electrical interference, so our bodies also need to be grounded.

Because these days we are insulated from the earth with our plastic and rubber soled shoes and gloves and even the carpets in our homes, alongside the fact that in modern society we have little opportunity nor need to touch the earth, then it is even more important for us to ground the body at least once a day.

With the advent of cell phones and computers the air around us is full of microwave radiation, telephone signals, smart meter signals, Internet signals etc.

The result of all this can be a disruption of our natural electrical condition and this could lead to allergies and ill health and also to undermining the immune system.

Because grounding increases the surface charge of red blood cells, this helps prevent clumping of the cells (which can lead to infarcts or blockages of the blood vessels resulting in stroke, heart attack etc.)

Other claims for earthing include faster healing of body wounds, better sleep, reduced inflammation and therefore improved mood. Inflammation often results in having a foggy mind, irritability, fatigue and mood swings. Further, earthing can result in faster recovery after exercising, reduce pain, reduce blood pressure, and provide more energy in general. Earthing has been shown also to steady the pulse rate.

Bear in mind that it is possible to purchase earthing sheets for your bed and also earthing footwear such as sandals and shoes.

## Contact with trees.

Because of their ability to absorb $CO_2$ and pollutants from the air and to breathe out life-giving oxygen, to capture and filter stormwater, to provide shade from the blistering sun, to provide habitats for wild animals and birds, as well as through their roots providing stability for the ground, trees are regarded as essential for the health of the whole planet.

Furthermore their fruits provide us with food and they can also be used in a warm fireplace as fuel. There are also many drugs which have derived from trees such as aspirin and tamoxifen.

On the level of emotional healing trees are said to reduce stress by reducing the levels of the stress hormone cortisol. It is said that people living in areas with trees are less depressed, have fewer negative thoughts, fewer low moods and they're more satisfied with their lives. In areas where there are many trees doctors prescribe fewer antidepressants.

By removing pollutants such as hydrocarbons, sulphur dioxide, nitrogen dioxide, and ozone, trees help to reduce the incidence of high blood pressure, heart failure, glaucoma, bronchitis and reduced cognitive development in children.

As mentioned in the section on grounding, contact with trees and plants in general can help to rebalance the electron density within the human body. This feel good factor may account for the popularity of tree hugging amongst nature loving people.

### Forest bathing. (Shinrin-Yoku).

In the early 80's, when technological development was booming, the Japanese government recognized the stresses of the modern world upon their people. Most of their population was living in overcrowded apartments and cities and so the Japanese national parks proposed a program which would counter the negative effects of living in tightly packed polluted cities.

As well as breathing in clean forest air and benefitting from the exercise (see previously – "emptying the emotional bucket), another main principle was to stimulate all of the five senses whilst walking in the forest.

You hear the birds and the animals, you can touch the trees or even walk barefoot, your sense of sight is delighted and enlivened by the various shades of greens and other colours in the forest; if you wish you can even taste those berries, nuts, flowers and leaves *which are safe to eat*, as you walk through the forest, and of course there is a very refreshing and stimulating aroma in the forest air.

In Japan this is known as a "forest shower".

It's claimed that breathing fresh forest air stimulates the immune system and increases the numbers of "natural killer cells" [same family as B and T type lymphocytes] as well as anti-cancer proteins. According to researcher Dr. Qing Li it is also important for us to stop and breathe deeply from time to time. Laboratory tests on the blood of volunteers have shown that the beneficial effects of forest bathing on the immune system can last up to a month.

Further, a walk in the forest reduces anxiety, anger, depression, fatigue and confusion. At the same time it increases our vigour.

To sum up, a walk in the forest once a week or even once a month has immense benefits on your physical, emotional and even on your spiritual health.

*Helping You Through Loss and Bereavement*

It must be emphasised that whatever advice is given in this book regarding walks and visits etcetera, you must *Please* ensure your own safety.

I am very fortunate to live on the edge of a wood and be surrounded by broad leaved trees within a 5 minute walk of my home. I only wish that this were possible for everyone.

# CHAPTER 3

# Emotional Health.

---※---

I have explained above how to empty your emotional bucket. Now it is time to look at the importance of family, friends and community.

The importance of human contact cannot be over-emphasised. Are you able to receive at least one hug a day?

Do you have family or friends? Can you arrange to see them or hear from them once a day?

Are you part of an association, group, church, synagogue, mosque or club whereby you can meet people? These days many groups such as book clubs, historical interest groups etc. meet on Zoom and this is a good alternative to in-person meetings such as bowls, tennis, golf clubs or for worship.

If receiving human touch is not possible for you how about treating yourself to a sauna and massage, Colour and Light Healing, Indian Head Massage, Reiki, Sound Healing, Aromatherapy or Osteopathic treatment where you will receive touch and conversation from and with another human being. There are numerous "alternative" therapies available these days and it is important to treat yourself and choose one or two to your liking.

Other options to improve emotional health include meditation, yoga and mindfulness classes.

Finally let us take a look at some Herbal, Bach Flower Remedies and Homeopathic supplements which are recommended for those in grief.

[Before doing so it should be noted that if you are suffering from severe depression, anxiety, severe lack of sleep etc. a visit to your health professional would be wise.]

The following is a brief overview of these alternative therapies and so a visit to a professional in the preferred treatment(s) is advisable.

Please ensure that the plants have not been sprayed with pesticides before picking.

## Herbal Remedies.

Hawthorne.

Hawthorne affects mainly the cardiovascular system and research shows it reduces cholesterol levels and high blood pressure.

It is a member of the rose family and is a main healer for heartache and grief.

You can make teas out of the berries, flowers and leaves.

Motherwort;

Is said to be effective in treating anxiety and stress. It may be especially helpful for grieving mothers or for those who have lost their mother.

As it has a bitter taste, it is advisable to add some sweeter content, such as honey, in order to make a tea out of its flowers and leaves.

Rose;

Is said to have antidepressant and sedative effects which result in relaxation and a better mood.

Supporting the nervous and digestive systems, Rose can reduce inflammation and feelings of anger (which are very common in the bereaved).

Rose can improve our self esteem and also improve our relationships with others.

Rose leaves, buds, flowers and hips are all beneficial and can be taken in the form of a tea.

Mimosa;

Known as "the tree of happiness" Mimosa is said to help with loss, heartache, grief and depression. It is also said to have a powerful grounding effect for those being swayed by powerful emotions and its bark and flowers can be infused into a tea.

Linden;

Is said to reduce the effects of stress, particularly high blood pressure, through its antioxidant nature.

For those in grief a Linden tea of leaves and flowers, can result in a protective and comforting effect.

Tulsi;

At this time you will need a boost to your energy and vitality and wellbeing. "Holy Basil" is the herb for you!

Tulsi supports the cardiovascular, nervous, digestive and immune systems.

Tea infused with its flowers and leaves can reduce the sense of hopelessness and increase harmony in our lives.

## Bach Flower Remedies.

As you will know many emotions arise during the bereavement journey. Guilt, anger, sadness, resentment, disbelief, loneliness, numbness and shock are some of the more common emotions . See how the following remedies can help with your emotions.

The Bach flower remedies are often used to support emotional well-being. Each of the 38 Bach flower remedies address a different emotion. Probably the best approach for you is to talk with someone who has been working with these remedies for a number of years. Their advice would be invaluable.

Here is an overview;

For shock, hopelessness and grief; *Star of Bethlehem* is used.

For anxiety; *Impatiens* is used (for a quick recovery), as well as *Mimulus*.

For anger; The use of *Holly* remedy is said to replace the anger with feelings of love and gentleness.

For guilt *pine* is used as well as *crab apple flower essence*.

For regrets and dwelling on the past use *Honeysuckle*.

For self pity and a tendency to complain and blame, *Willow* is used.

For loneliness; *Water Violet, Heather, and Impatiens* are used.

For those who are feeling depressed and despondent without joy or energy, the *Mustard flower* is said to restore these latter uplifting qualities.

## Homeopathic remedies.

Homeopathy can provide a gentle and safe alternative to conventional medicines which may simply mask the symptoms. Homeopathy can strengthen your resilience and ability to cope.

As with all health treatments it is best to seek out a professional with a good knowledge and experience of their craft for advice.

After the loss, when you are stuck in grief and cannot get out of that state **Ignatia** may be of help. You may have periods of crying uncontrollably, find it hard to speak of your loss and you may prefer to be alone. Little things may cause angry outbursts or a lump in the throat. You may suffer from digestive problems, headaches and anxiety.

When you feel alone and abandoned and this causes a tearful and distressed condition **Pulsatilla** may be of help. You may be looking for sympathy and support and may simply want to be held by another.

If you are lacking in energy and feel exhausted yet cannot sleep because of anxiety you may benefit from **Phosphoric acid**. After the initial period of grief has passed, you may feel isolated. Difficulty in concentrating and headache may also be present.

If you are one who likes to keep their feelings private and to be crying alone, **Nat Mur** may help. It is difficult for others to approach and support you as you are very private and would prefer not to cause any fuss. You may feel betrayed and hurt and have a tendency to dwell on the past.

Those who are experienced in the use of the above natural remedies are certain they will help support you through your grieving process.

# CHAPTER 4

# Spiritual Health.

---※---

Guided meditation; 20 mins; (this will be available as spoken word on Audible but for paperback or hard cover readers, please visualise and memorise the following);

"Find yourself a quiet space, somewhere where you won't be disturbed, ensure all the phones are turned off and any noise from television or radio in the background is turned off.

This may mean rising early in the morning before anyone else gets up, or going to bed 20 minutes later than everyone else. However, this time put aside will be very beneficial for you.

Sit comfortably, with your back fairly straight but relaxed.

Close your eyes then feel your feet on the floor. Remain focussed on your feet for a couple of minutes. Taking the attention and energy away from the head to the feet will slow down any distracting thoughts.

Now slowly bring your attention up to the lower legs, relaxing any tensions as you go, and travel slowly up the body, knees, thighs, pelvis, abdomen, chest and arms, relaxing any tensions you may find.

When you reach the neck, imagine a space there, a bubble, and extend this bubble to include the chest. This will help prevent unwanted words and conversations showing up in your mind.

Finally relax the muscles of the face, eyes, back of the head and bring your attention to the top of the head. From here become aware of your body as a whole.

Now imagine yourself in your favourite valley, with high mountains either side, a river and streams, woodlands and forests and a small road running through the valley.

The sun is shining and the sky is blue and, thankfully, there are a few clouds here and there so that it doesn't feel uncomfortably hot.

You decide to climb a nearby mountain in order to gain a clearer view of the landscape and of your life.

You have no map as you make your way through the woods along a narrow path toward the mountain.

You encounter fallen trees and branches, brambles and stinging nettles as you go, but gradually the land begins to rise and soon you are out of the forest and on the lower slopes of the mountain.

You may feel your breath quickening as the track gradually becomes steeper but as you look back you can see well above the trees, and the lower parts of the valley become clearer.

As you continue to climb, you feel the air is cooler but the view of the valley below and the surrounding mountains is much clearer.

You are glad you tied your sweater around your waist and now put it on as you pause to sit on a smooth rock.

Not far to go now to the top of the mountain and as you get nearer your excitement grows, you quicken your pace, your breathing accelerates and finally you reach the highest point.

Imagine a roar releasing itself from your throat, loud and clear, full of emotion..

It feels as though the whole valley can hear you and (inwardly) you keep shouting at the top of your lungs, until your voice and emotions have run out.

Looking around you see many, many mountain peaks, some lower and some higher than yours. You feel physically and emotionally tired, but in a good way. There is still plenty of daylight for the descent and you take a cool drink of pure water from a nearby spring.

Down below you know the farms are full of activity as the farmers tend their animals and crops. A few cars scurry along the country road - perhaps on their way to a distant town for an afternoon shift or to the shops.

Up here though all is at peace. You bathe in the silence and stillness, place your seating pad on a smooth rock, sit and close your eyes.

In your mind's eye you see others on the top of the mountain, some who've only recently passed away.

Your heart opens and love rays out from you and envelops those around you.

The love keeps spreading until the whole creation is full of love.

*Helping You Through Loss and Bereavement*

You realise the universe is One and that you can never be separated from the ones you love, whether they are in their bodies, or have left their bodies.

You feel pure bliss and want everyone to feel this way.

In your mind's eye you see that everyone is on their own journey, some going up the mountains, up the rough and steep slopes and some going up the easy way, spiralling around the mountain and taking more time.

Now you notice those coming down, they appear to be very young, innocent and rather unsure. Some end up in the broad fields, others in the brambles and have to find their way out, others in small boats floating on the little streams, having quite an easy ride.

Upon the mountain top, gradually, you begin to feel your body again as the air grows chilly and it is time to return to the valley".

*In your own time feel your feet, your hands and fingers and gently rub your hands together, then place your palms over your eyes.*

*Open your eyes when you are ready."*

This guided meditation can be used at any time you and will bring you relaxation and a greater feeling of peace.

If you are a member of a particular religion then don't hesitate to contact your priest. They are very experienced in dealing with bereavements and should be able to give you good, solid support.

# CHAPTER 5

# The stages of grief and two models of grief.

―❦―

Just a few words on the stages of grief. The bereavement service CRUSE give 5 stages of grief as follows; denial, anger, bargaining, depression and acceptance.

These stages don't always appear in this order and the main point here is to assure you that *whatever you are feeling is OK.*

There is no standard way of grieving. Every individual grieves in a different way and with different timings.

Let's take a look at the above stages in the order in which they are said to appear;

1. Denial. Soon after hearing of the death of a loved one you may experience a sense of disbelief and what has been described as numbness.

*A personal anecdote here;*

*My best friend Richard passed away several years ago at quite a young age. I received a phone call out of the blue from an acquaintance of Richard's who left an almost hysterical message on the voicemail to the effect that he had passed away unexpectedly and suddenly.*

*My initial reaction was total disbelief. I knew I had to acknowledge the death of my friend but had no idea what to do next. I decided the choice was between a walk along the banks of the sacred river Dee in North Wales, near to where I lived or to visit the nearby, beautiful stone circle of Moel Ty Uchaf, one of my favourite places. I decided on the latter and walked up to the circle, gradually ascending the incline. This gave me time to not only acknowledge the death of my friend but also to begin the grieving process. I believe that walking and becoming a bit breathless on the journey helped this process of coming to terms with the sudden death. Nevertheless it took some time for my mind to accept that my friend had passed away. Denial is very common in the early stages and you will need to give yourself time to come to terms with your loss.*

## 2. Anger.

You may feel angry at the world for taking your loved one away especially if this is a premature death and your beloved has died young. It may be that your beloved attended the hospital before death and I have known clients who have been furious with the doctors and nurses at the hospital and some even have gone on to sue the health service.

My advice to these clients was always to write down their angry thoughts to their full extent leaving nothing out, as though they were sending that letter of complaint to the hospital, or to whomever they felt was responsible for the death of their beloved one.

When they had completed the letter, and this may take several days, my advice to them was not to send it to the hospital but to burn it and to give themselves time to consider what had happened from a less emotional position.

It's always good in these cases to discuss with someone you trust the emotions and the pain you are feeling and to get their advice as an objective third party as to what to do next.

*This is particularly important if you are blaming and angry at yourself for not doing enough for the deceased. With the help of a good friend you may come to see that what you did was more than enough and that there would have been nothing more that a reasonable person could have done. You were probably unaware and not in control of many factors.*

## 3. Bargaining.

You feel bad. You want to get out of this sad situation. You bargain with God, with Life, with yourself.

"If I behave in a certain way, will you make the pain disappear?"

This is a natural response to suffering as you feel helpless and unable to control the situation, but don't let the "monkey mind" take over!

## 4. Depression.

The first three stages above can take place within a benumbed and foggy mind. Once it becomes obvious that Bargaining is not an option, the clarity gained can result in a more intense feeling of Grief, as the reality hits home. For some it is an opportunity to move on to Acceptance, but for others it may lead to self-imposed isolation and greater inwardness.

If this becomes severe and is not alleviated by natural means, then it may require a period of anti-depressant medicines under the guidance of your medical practitioner.

## 5. Acceptance and hope.

At this stage you come to terms with the fact that your life, relationship and future direction have changed significantly. You are well beyond the stage of denial and now are investigating and coping with the new reality which faces you after the bereavement.

A new life lies ahead and you might be feeling more relaxed, optimistic, more present during your daily activities, caring for yourself and understanding that emotions and grief are natural and recurring, temporary, phenomena throughout our lives.

Your memory is now more focussed on the good times you shared with the deceased rather than your own pain and grief.

At this stage you may be visiting the grave or plot at regular intervals and may be sharing anecdotes and happy memories with friends and family. You may wish to celebrate important events and dates in the life of the deceased and you find that this becomes a new habit and one to be treasured.

**KÜBLER-ROSS GRIEF CYCLE**

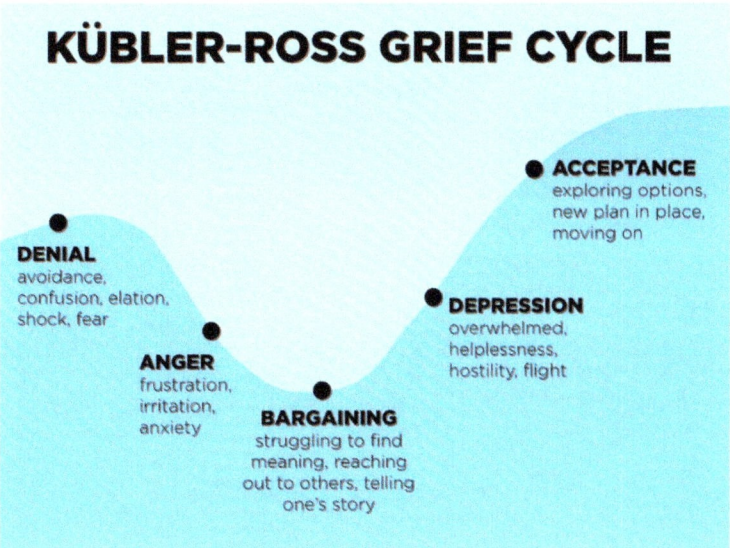

**DENIAL**
avoidance,
confusion, elation,
shock, fear

**ANGER**
frustration,
irritation,
anxiety

**BARGAINING**
struggling to find
meaning, reaching
out to others, telling
one's story

**DEPRESSION**
overwhelmed,
helplessness,
hostility, flight

**ACCEPTANCE**
exploring options,
new plan in place,
moving on

## Two models of the Grief journey;

[a] The Dual Process model.

This model supposes two aspects; the loss-orientated, which deals with the past, and the restoration-orientated, dealing with the future.

The idea is that the bereaved moves back and forth between these two aspects, dealing with the funeral etc. from the past and with new situations, financial, social etc. in the future.

I should like to propose a third state, where the bereaved forgets for a while the above two aspects and simply lives in the present, taking a breather, even enjoying life!

**Everyday life experience**

**Loss-oriented**

Grief work
Intrusion of grief
Relinquishing-continuing-relocating bonds / ties
Denial/avoidance of restoration changes

**Restoration-oriented**

Attending to life changes
Doing new things
Distraction from grief
Denial/avoidance of grief
New roles/ identities/ relationships

*oscillation*

## [b] The Tonkin Model.

The idea of "growing around" grief has the advantage of being both simple and objective.

In the 1990's, Dr.Tonkin was working as a counsellor when he met a client who had lost a child many years previously. They had both expected grief to lessen with time but the way she described, and drew it, showed that, whereas her grief was all-encompassing at the beginning, taking over every aspect of her life, as time went on and her life expanded, the grief became smaller *in proportion*. This simple concept can give hope for the bereaved.

*David Griffiths*

# Tonkin's Model of Grief

Growing around grief

Your life

Time

Grief

Grief

Grief

# CHAPTER 6

# Grief and Bereavement as significant stages on the spiritual path.

---

The experience of loss can have a massive effect on your life path, though it may be that what you seek is a return to the life you had before bereavement, and this is fine.

Most bereavement counsellors see this as their objective, that is to return the clients back to "normality". The client sees this as their objective also.

However for a few people the events of loss and death cause such a shake up in their inner life that they start to ask questions which they may never have asked in their lives before, especially if they experience very painful grief.

It's not unusual for the bereaved to question whether the soul and spirit of the deceased has now moved on to another reality. They may start to investigate world religions or spiritual texts to see what they have to say about life after death. They may watch YouTube videos on near-death experiences to find out what these people experienced on the "other side" before coming back.

Other questions which may arise during the period of grief are; what's the point of it all?, why am I here?, what's this world all about?

For many these serious questions may be shocking. What are the answers? Does anyone have the answers? Can I do anything myself in order to find the answers?

The period of intense grief can lead to a change in consciousness; the world is empty and grey, communication is shallow and as though there are clouds between you and the world, life has no meaning, people have no meaning, their activities are meaningless, your own activities have no meaning. This is how it can feel.

Although at the time this is an incredibly painful experience it can have a hidden benefit, inasmuch as your consciousness is shaken up it can open you to new experiences, new states of consciousness.

If you practice the exercise on sitting with your beloved who has passed, with a table and candle and letters, and other items that belonged to them, you will find that the focus upon the deceased and the feeling of their presence is in itself a profound change of consciousness. You may never have felt so much stillness and so much peace in your life before this. Your thoughts may have slowed down or even come to a complete standstill, your concentration is at a high pitch, although never forced. Your listening is intense.

If this is the case for you, you may well be ready to start on a meditative path.

Which path you take will depend on how attracted you are to that school or to that teacher. For me it was a great fortune in my life to discover Richard Stevens, Samuel Sagan, Sadhguru and Wendell Henckel.

Whilst it's not a good idea to flit from one teacher to another, it can work in some cases where one develops certain capacities with one teacher and moves on to other capacities with the next.

At the end of the day progress relies upon the ability to remain still and silent. If you follow the practices given by Sadhguru, Mooji, the Clairvision School and others, you will eventually come to awareness in the present moment. There follows the realization that thoughts, memories and imaginations about the future all exist within the present. There is no future and there was no past.

**Everything exists Now.**

*Then you come to realise that, in essence, you can never be separate from your beloved.*

..........................

(If you are someone who does not feel attracted to having a spiritual teacher, you might wish to look into a Mindfulness practice and here is a link to some excellent audio meditations: http://www.sharingmindfulness.com/audio/)

Although we are coming to the end of this book *this is not the end of support for you.* Just remember you're not alone, there is always someone out there that you can call on and the list in the next chapter gives you some agencies which can help with various aspects of bereavement and grief as well as other aspects of the bereavement journey.

I shall soon be publishing another book which deals with the practicalities following the death of someone you cared for.

If you wish to be informed of the publication date of this book and of other books on bereavement which I shall be publishing, please send an e-mail to this address;

dgwesternshores@mail.com

It may be that you know someone who has been bereaved and needs such a book as this and you may wish to present it as a gift to them.

*Helping You Through Loss and Bereavement*

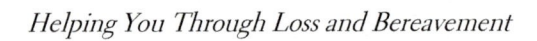

Thank you for reading this book and my dearest wish is that it has, and will, help to support you through one of the most painful periods of your life, following the death of a very special loved one.

# CHAPTER 7

# Helpful links

---

**Bereavement support services.**

Marie Curie; [When someone dies (mariecurie.org.uk)](#)

[Child Bereavement UK](#) – offers support if you are bereaved after losing a child. Or if you're a child or young person who is grieving after losing someone.

At a Loss – find bereavement services and counselling across the UK, including resources on bereavement during the pandemic.

[Cruse Bereavement Support](#) – offers face-to-face, telephone, email and online support for anyone who has experienced a loss.

[The Compassionate Friends](#) – find support for bereaved parents and their families, including a helpline.

[The Good Grief Trust](#) – a charity run by bereaved people, helping all those experiencing grief in the UK. Provides information and stories about grief and bereavement, including a [map of UK bereavement services](#).

[Hub of Hope](#) – database of mental health services in the UK, including community, charity, private and NHS mental health support.

*Helping You Through Loss and Bereavement*

Dying Matters – resources to help people talk more openly about dying, death and bereavement, and to make plans for the end of life.

WAY (Widowed and Young) – advice for people who have lost a partner before their 51st birthday.

Samaritans – if you're struggling you can call Samaritans any time on 116 123 to talk about anything. You can also email them at jo@samaritans.org. Or contact them by post at Freepost SAMARITANS LETTERS. Samaritans also have a Welsh Language Line on 0808 164 0123 (7pm–11pm every day).

Sands – information and support for anybody affected by the death of a baby. Support includes a helpline and live chat.

Sue Ryder – offers bereavement support, including ways of finding bereavement support online.

**Financial advice.**

MoneyHelper offers free, impartial advice backed by the UK Government. It offers money and pensions guidance online, over the phone or in person and can connect you to a free debt adviser.

So, whether you're looking to make the most of your money, cut your debt or even plan ahead or find out whether you're entitled to any benefits, MoneyHelper can offer helpful guidance.

StepChange is the UK's leading debt charity and has helped millions of people deal with their debt problems for free.

You can get advice online or over the phone. StepChange will help you work out your income, budget and debts and use this to devise a solution before setting up a plan and extra support.

Citizens Advice offers free, independent advice in various areas, including guidance on pensions, housing, employment issues, debt, benefits, family matters and consumer rights.

The organisation's network of independent charities can give confidential advice over the phone, online or in person.

Citizens Advice says it helped solve the problems of 75% of people it directly gave advice to last year.

The Financial Ombudsman helps settle complaints about financial businesses for free.

They may be able to help if you have any issues with:

- Financial advice, pensions and investments
- Bank accounts, payments and cards
- Insurance products
- Loans and finance loans
- Debt collection and repayment problems

## National Debtline

Run by the Money Advice Trust, National Debtline is a free and confidential debt advice service.

You can either call, use its online webchat or use the digital advice tool to get the right advice for you.

*Helping You Through Loss and Bereavement*

If you're struggling with your finances and are not sure where to turn, it's worth getting in touch with a trusted organisation that can offer free, impartial and confidential advice.

# CHAPTER 8

# Poems and writings about grief and loss.

---⋆---

### Do not stand.

Do not stand at my grave and weep
I am not there. I do not sleep.
I am 1000 winds that blow.
I am the diamond glints on snow.
I am the sunlight on ripened grain.
I am the gentle autumn rain.
When you awaken in the morning's hush
I am the swift uplifting rush
Of quiet birds in circled flight.
I am the soft stars that shine at night.
Do not stand at my grave and cry;
I am not there. I did not die

Anonymous.

### All is Well.

Death is nothing at all,
I have only slipped into the next room
I am I and you are you
Whatever we were to each other, that we are still.
Call me by my old familiar name,
Speak to me in the easy way which you always used

Put no difference in your tone,
Wear no forced air of solemnity or sorrow.
Laugh as we always laughed at the little jokes
we enjoyed together.
Play, smile, think of me, pray for me.
Let my name be ever the household word that
It always was,
Let it be spoken without effect, without the
Trace of shadow on it.
Life means all that it ever meant.
It is the same as it ever was, there is unbroken
Continuity.
Why should I be out of mind because I am out
Of sight?
I am waiting for you, for an interval,
Somewhere very near,
Just around the corner,
All is well.

Henry Scott Holland.

## When I'm gone.

When I come to the end of my journey
And I travel my last weary mile
Just forget it if you can, That I ever frowned
And Remember only the smile
Forget unkind words i have spoken
Remember Some good I have done
Forget that I ever had heartache

*David Griffiths*

And Remember I've had loads of fun
Forget that I've stumbled and blundered
And sometimes fell by the way
Remember I have fought some hard battles
And won, ere The close of day
Then forget to grieve for my going
I would not have you sad for a day
But in summer just gather some flowers
And remember the place where I lay
And come in the shade of evening
When the sun paints the sky in the West
Stand for a few moments beside me
And remember only my best.


Mosiah Lyman Hancock

**A happy man.**

When these graven lines you see,
Traveler do not pity me;
Though I be among the dead,
Let no Bourne-full word be said.

Children that I leave behind,
And their children, all were kind;
Near to them and to my wife,
I was happy all my life.

My three sons I married right,
And their sons I rocked at night;

Death nor sorrow never brought
Cause for one unhappy thought.

Now, and with no need of tears,
Here they leave me, full of years,~~
Leave me to my quiet rest
In the region of the blest.

Edwin Arlington Robinson.

## When I Die.

When I die
when my coffin
is being taken out
you must never think
i am missing this world

don't shed any tears
don't lament or
feel sorry
i'm not falling
into a monster's abyss

when you see
my corpse is being carried
don't cry for my leaving
i'm not leaving
i'm arriving at eternal love

*David Griffiths*

when you leave me
in the grave
don't say goodbye
remember a grave is
only a curtain
for the paradise behind

you'll only see me
descending into a grave
now watch me rise
how can there be an end
when the sun sets or
the moon goes down

it looks like the end
it seems like a sunset
but in reality it is a dawn
when the grave locks you up
that is when your soul is freed

have you ever seen
a seed fallen to earth
not rise with a new life
why should you doubt the rise
of a seed named human

have you ever seen
a bucket lowered into a well
coming back empty

why lament for a soul
when it can come back
like Joseph from the well

when for the last time
you close your mouth
your words and soul
will belong to the world of
no place no time.

Kahlil Gibran..

"I'm There Inside Your Heart" by Unknown

Right now I'm in a different place
And though we seem apart
I'm closer than I ever was,
I'm there inside your heart.

I'm with you when you greet each day
And while the sun shines bright
I'm there to share the sunsets, too
I'm with you every night.

I'm with you when the times are good
To share a laugh or two,
And if a tear should start to fall
I'll still be there for you.

*David Griffiths*

And when that day arrives
That we no longer are apart,
I'll smile and hold you close to me,
Forever in my heart.

Let Me Go.

When I come to the end of the road
And the sun has set for me
I want no rites in a gloom filled room
Why cry for a soul set free?

Miss me a little, but not for long
And not with your head bowed low
Remember the love that once we shared
Miss me, but let me go.

For this is a journey we all must take
And each must go alone.
It's all part of the master plan
A step on the road to home.

When you are lonely and sick at heart
Go to the friends we know.
Laugh at all the things we used to do
Miss me, but let me go.

Christina Georgina Rossetti

There are many more poems of course on the subject of death and dying, grief and bereavement. I have published a volume containing such poems. If required, chosen poems can then be read out at a funeral service.

Printed in Great Britain
by Amazon